INTERNATIONAL CUISINE SERIES

Vegetarian

CHINESE Cooking

Sanjeev Kapoor's

INTERNATIONAL CUISINE SERIES

Vegetarian

CHINESE Cooking

Sanjeev Kapoor's

In association with Alyona Kapoor

Popular
Prakashan
www.popularprakashan.com

POPULAR PRAKASHAN PVT. LTD.
301 Mahalaxmi Chambers
22, Bhulabhai Desai Road
Mumbai - 400026

First Published 2007

(4057)
ISBN- 81-7991- 309-0

Design: Creative Quotient
(CQ-A Repro India Limited Enterprise)

Published by Ramdas Bhatkal
for Popular Prakashan Pvt. Ltd.
301, Mahalaxmi Chambers
22, Bhulabhai Desai Road
Mumbai – 400026

DEDICATION

To my readers and fellow-travellers on a
gastronomical tour of the great cuisines of the world.
May we continue to discover and experience together
the unique flavours of many lands.

AUTHOR'S NOTE

Chinese food has become so much a part of the Indian culinary scene that one would be forgiven for thinking of it as just another one of India's many regional foods. We have so adapted Chinese cuisine to suit our Indian palates, as to make it practically unrecognisable in the land of its origin, in the process creating a whole new cuisine which has gained popularity the world over as "Indian Chinese"!

This new book attempts to give you an experience of authentic Chinese cuisine from the many different regions of China, and includes some of our popular Indian versions as well. Like India, China's vast lands are host to many different cultures and food styles, like the bland but flavourful cuisine of the Cantonese region, home of dim sum; or the red cooking of Shanghai, considered the gastronomical capital of China. But the Chinese cuisines most similar to our own Indian Chinese versions are from the Sichuan and Hunan regions. Sichuan dishes like Sichuan Vegetables are characterised by a liberal use of ginger, garlic and Sichuan pepper, which is neither a peppercorn, nor a chilli, but a berry and cousin of our own "tirphal". The food of the Hunan region with its hot and sour flavours and use of chillies and shallots also finds great resonance in India.

Underlying the regional differences, however, is a philosophy of food, which is the unifying element in all Chinese cooking. Foods have been classified into Yin (cooling foods) and

Yang (hot foods). The Chinese believe that Yin and Yang, symbolised by two interlocking shapes within a circle, are not limited to foods, but infuse every aspect of our lives.

Another important element in the preparation of food is the Chinese concept of Five. Apart from the familiar 5-spice powder, Chinese cooking acknowledges the importance of the traditional five flavours: sweet, sour, bitter, hot and salty, to which have now been added xiang (aromatic) and xian (savoury). The perfect Chinese dish would achieve a balance and contrast in different flavours, colours, textures and aromas and ultimately contribute to the well-being of the consumer.

The secret to cooking Chinese food however, lies in the preparation and freshness of the ingredients. Ingredients of varying textures are cut in contrasting or complimentary shapes and sizes, and marinated or readied just in time for use. Many Chinese dishes require stir-frying on high heat to maintain their crispness and freshness. For dishes that are braised, stewed or boiled, ingredients are added according to their cooking times to ensure they retain their texture. The emphasis is on healthy and wholesome cooking which engages all the senses for maximum pleasure.

In the words of an ancient Chinese proverb, *"A good meal is eaten first with the eyes, then with the nose and finally with the mouth."*

With this book as your guide, I wish you many happy hours of preparing and enjoying this ancient, aromatic and flavourful cuisine in your own home.

ACKNOWLEDGEMENTS

Anand Bhandiwad
Anil Bhandari
Anupa Das
Asha Madhavan
Ashlesha Shirodkar
Bhartendu Sharma
Drs. Meena & Ram Prabhoo
Gajendra Mule
Ganesh Pednekar
Harpal Singh Sokhi
Jaideep Chaubal
Jyotsna & Mayur Dvivedi
Kruti Kotak
Lohana Khaandaan
Mahendra Ghanekar
Mrs. Lata Lohana & Capt. K. K. Lohana

Namrata & Sanjiv Bahl
Neelima Acharya
Neena Murdeshwar
Pooja & Rajeev Kapoor
Prachi Hatwalne
Raj Rege
Rajeev Matta
Rita D'Souza
Rutika Samtani
Saurabh Mishra
Shishir Chachad
Shivani Ganesh
Smeeta Bhatkal
Swapna Shinde
Tripta Bhagattjee
Vinayak Gawande

CONTENTS

CLEAR LEMON CORIANDER SOUP

Ingredients

2¾ teaspoons lemon juice

½ teaspoon grated lemon rind

3 tablespoons fresh coriander leaves,
   finely chopped

1 medium carrot, cut into ½-inch pieces

2-3 baby corn cobs, cut into ½-inch pieces

¼ small head broccoli, separated
   into florets

1 tablespoon oil

1 spring onion, chopped

2 garlic cloves, finely chopped

¼ small Chinese cabbage, cut into
   ½-inch pieces

2-3 fresh button mushrooms, sliced

4 cups Vegetable Stock (*page 104*)

salt to taste

4-5 black peppercorns, freshly crushed

¼ teaspoon MSG (optional)

Method

1   Blanch carrot, baby corn and broccoli in boiling water for one minute. Drain, refresh in cold water and set aside.

2   Heat oil in a wok; add spring onion and garlic and sauté on medium heat for half a minute. Add the Chinese cabbage and mushrooms and stir-fry on high heat for two minutes. Stir in the vegetable stock and bring to a boil.

3   Add the blanched vegetables and cook on high heat for one minute. Stir in salt, crushed peppercorns, lemon rind and MSG, and continue cooking for another minute.

4   Add lemon juice and fresh coriander leaves. Stir to mix and serve hot.

HOT AND SOUR VEGETABLE SOUF

Ingredients

1 slice bamboo shoot

½ medium carrot, grated

¼ small cabbage, finely chopped

2 fresh button mushrooms, finely chopped

½ medium green capsicum, finely chopped

4-6 French beans, finely chopped

2 tablespoons oil

1 small onion, finely chopped

2-3 garlic cloves, finely chopped

1 inch ginger, grated

2-inch celery stalk, finely chopped

½ teaspoon white pepper powder

salt to taste

½ teaspoon sugar

¼ teaspoon MSG (optional)

2 tablespoons soy sauce

2 tablespoons green chilli sauce

4-5 cups Vegetable Stock (*page104*)

3 tablespoons cornflour

2 tablespoons white vinegar

1 tablespoon Chilli Oil (*page 100*)

1 stalk spring onion greens, finely chopped

Method

1   Boil the bamboo shoot in one cup of water for two to three minutes. Drain and chop fine.

2   Heat oil in a wok or saucepan; add onion, garlic and ginger and stir-fry for one minute. Add bamboo shoot, carrot, cabbage, mushrooms, green capsicum, French beans and celery. Cook stirring continuously for two to three minutes, or until vegetables are almost cooked.

3   Add white pepper powder, salt to taste, sugar, MSG, soy sauce, green chilli sauce and mix well.

4   Stir in the vegetable stock and bring to a boil. Mix cornflour with half a cup of water and stir into the soup. Cook, stirring continuously, for one minute or until the soup thickens.

5   Stir in the vinegar, drizzle the chilli oil over and serve piping hot, garnished with chopped spring onion greens.

━━━━━━━ CHEF'S TIP ━━━━━━━

We have used tinned bamboo shoots which are preserved in brine, hence they have to be boiled in water before use.

(see picture on page 102)

SWEET CORN VEGETABLE SOUP

Ingredients

½ cup sweet corn kernels

150 grams cream-style sweet corn

¼ small cabbage, finely chopped

¼ medium carrot, finely diced

3 tablespoons cornflour

2 tablespoons oil

4-5 cups Vegetable Stock (*page 104*)

salt to taste

¼ teaspoon white pepper powder

½ tablespoon sugar

¼ teaspoon MSG (optional)

1 stalk spring onion greens, chopped

Method

1   Heat oil in a wok or pan; add corn kernels, cabbage and carrot and stir-fry for a couple of minutes. Stir in the vegetable stock and bring to a boil.

2   Mix in the cream-style sweet corn and continue cooking for two to three minutes, or until well mixed. Mix cornflour and half a cup of water.

3   Add salt, white pepper powder, sugar and MSG. Stir in the cornflour mixture and cook, stirring continuously on high heat for one minute, or until the soup has thickened.

4   Serve piping hot, garnished with the chopped spring onion greens.

VEGETABLE NOODLE SOUP

Ingredients

4-5 fresh button mushrooms, finely sliced

1 medium carrot, grated

½ medium green capsicum, cut into thin strips

8-10 spinach leaves, finely shredded

40 grams eggless noodles

1 tablespoon oil

2-3 garlic cloves, crushed

1 dried red chilli, seeded and shredded

4-5 cups Vegetable Stock (*page 104*)

¼ teaspoon MSG (optional)

¼ teaspoon white pepper powder

salt to taste

1 tablespoon white vinegar

Method

1   Heat oil in a wok or pan; add garlic and stir-fry for half a minute. Add mushrooms, carrot and green capsicum and stir-fry for two minutes.

2   Add the red chilli and immediately stir in the stock.

3   Bring the mixture to a boil, add noodles, lower heat and simmer for three to four minutes, stirring occasionally.

4   Add MSG, white pepper powder and salt to taste.

5   Stir in the vinegar and shredded spinach leaves, cook for one minute and serve hot.

CHEF'S TIP

Vary the quantity of noodles to taste. To make a complete meal of this soup, increase the quantity of noodles and serve in a large bowl

CRISP PEPPER AND SALT VEGETABLES

Ingredients

3 baby corn cobs
3 fresh button mushrooms, halved
6 small heads broccoli, separated into
   small florets
½ small green capsicum, diced
½ small red capsicum, diced
½ small yellow capsicum, diced
50 grams bean curd (tofu), cubed
1 tablespoon oil + for deep-frying
½ inch ginger, finely chopped
2 garlic cloves, finely chopped
¼ celery stalk, finely chopped

salt to taste
5-6 black peppercorns, crushed
a small pinch of MSG (optional)
½ tablespoon dark soy sauce
½ teaspoon sugar
1 teaspoon white vinegar

Batter
¾ cup cornflour
6 tablespoons refined flour (*maida*)
½ teaspoon baking powder
salt to taste

Method

1   Blanch the baby corn in two cups of boiling water for two to three minutes. Drain and slice into rings.

2   Mix all the ingredients for the batter together with three-fourth cup plus one-and-a-half tablespoons of water and whisk with a balloon whisk to make a smooth batter.

3   Heat oil in a wok. Dip pieces of fried baby corn, mushroom, broccoli, green, red and yellow capsicum and tofu separately in the batter and deep-fry till golden and crisp. Drain on absorbent paper and set aside.

4   Heat one tablespoon of oil in a wok; add ginger and garlic and sauté on medium heat for half a minute.

5   Add celery and continue to sauté for half a minute more.

6   Add fried vegetables, tofu, salt, crushed peppercorns, MSG, dark soy sauce, sugar and vinegar and cook on high heat for one minute, tossing continuously. Serve hot.

CRISPY WONTONS

Ingredients

24 Wonton Wrappers (*page 26*)
2 tablespoons oil + for deep-frying
4-6 garlic cloves, finely chopped
2 spring onions, finely chopped
2 medium green capsicums, finely chopped
8-10 French beans, finely chopped
2 medium carrots, finely chopped
½ small cabbage, finely chopped
½ teaspoon white pepper powder
salt to taste
¼ teaspoon MSG (optional)
1 teaspoon light soy sauce

Method

1 Heat two tablespoons of oil in a wok or pan; add garlic and stir-fry for half a minute. Add spring onions, green capsicums, French beans, carrots and cabbage and continue to stir-fry for a couple of minutes more, stirring and tossing continuously.

2 Add white pepper powder, salt, MSG and soy sauce and cook for half a minute. Take the pan off the heat and allow the vegetables to cool.

3 Divide prepared filling into twenty-four equal portions. Place a portion of filling in the centre of each wonton wrapper; moisten the edges with a little water, fold in half diagonally, twist the ends and press lightly to stick together.

4 Heat oil in a wok and deep-fry the wontons for two to three minutes, or until crisp and golden brown. Drain on absorbent paper.

5 Serve hot with Sichuan Sauce (*page 102*).

CHEF'S TIP

For Wonton Wrappers, knead 2 cups of refined flour with ½ cup warm water to make a firm dough. Roll the dough into a large thin square sheet, about 1 mm thick. Cut into 3-inch squares and use as required.

Crispy Wonton

STEAMED MOMOS

Ingredients

1 cup refined flour (*maida*)
10 French beans, finely chopped
1 medium carrot, finely chopped
4-5 fresh button mushrooms,
  finely chopped
2 spring onions, finely chopped
¼ cup bean sprouts
8-10 cashew nuts, chopped
1 inch ginger, finely chopped
1 green chilli, finely chopped
8-10 black peppercorns, crushed

½ tablespoon light soy sauce
1 teaspoon sesame oil
¼ teaspoon MSG (optional)
salt to taste
1 stalk spring onion greens, chopped

Method

1 Mix refined flour with five tablespoons of water and knead into a stiff dough. Cover with a damp cloth and set aside for fifteen minutes.

2 In a large bowl, combine French beans, carrot, button mushrooms, spring onions, bean sprouts, cashew nuts, ginger, green chilli, peppercorns, soy sauce, sesame oil, MSG and salt to taste.

3 Divide the dough into sixteen equal portions and roll into thin small discs.

4 Place a spoonful of the vegetable filling in the centre of each disc and bring the sides together in the centre, pinching firmly together to form a dumpling.

5 Line a steamer with a clean, damp piece of muslin and arrange the momos in it.

6 Cover and steam for eight to ten minutes, until momos are cooked through.

7 Transfer to a serving plate. Garnish with spring onion greens and serve hot with Sichuan Sauce (*page 102*).

CRISPY BABY CORN

Ingredients

16 baby corn cobs

¼ cup cornflour

½ cup refined flour (*maida*)

¼ teaspoon baking powder

¼ teaspoon soda bicarbonate

salt to taste

½ tablespoon oil + for deep-frying

2-3 spring onions, chopped

2-3 tablespoons Sichuan Sauce (*page 102*)

2 stalks spring onion greens, chopped

Method

1   Blanch the baby corn in two cups of boiling water for two to three minutes. Drain.

2   Mix together cornflour, refined flour, baking powder, soda bicarbonate and salt. Stir in half a cup plus one tablespoon of water to make a moderately thick batter.

3   Heat oil in a wok; dip baby corn in the batter and deep-fry till light golden and crisp. Drain on absorbent paper.

4   Return the fried baby corn to the hot oil and fry once again till golden brown and crisp. Drain on absorbent paper and set aside.

5   Heat half a tablespoon of oil in a separate wok; add spring onions and Sichuan sauce and sauté on medium heat for half a minute.

6   Add fried baby corn and spring onion greens; cook on high heat for one minute, tossing continuously. Serve hot.

SICHUAN VEGETABLE FINGERS

Ingredients

1 medium carrot, grated

¼ medium cauliflower, grated

1 small green capsicum, finely chopped

¼ small cabbage, finely chopped

8-10 French beans, finely chopped

1 small onion, finely chopped

salt to taste

5 tablespoons cornflour

2 tablespoons refined four (*maida*)

2 teaspoons red chilli flakes

¼ teaspoon MSG (optional)

2 tablespoons fresh coriander leaves, finely chopped

¼ teaspoon white pepper powder

1 teaspoon light soy sauce

1 tablespoon oil + for deep-frying

Method

1 In a large bowl, combine carrot, cauliflower, capsicum, cabbage, French beans, onion and salt. Set aside for ten to fifteen minutes.

2 Squeeze the vegetables to remove excess water.

3 Add three tablespoons of cornflour, refined flour, red chilli flakes, MSG, coriander leaves, white pepper powder and soy sauce to the vegetables and mix well.

4 Divide this mixture into sixteen equal portions and roll into balls. Shape each ball into two-inch long fingers.Dust the vegetable fingers with two tablespoons of cornflour.

5 Heat oil in a wok and deep-fry the fingers till golden and crisp. Drain on absorbent paper.

6 Serve hot, with Sichuan Sauce.

CRACKLING SPINACH

Ingredients

45 spinach leaves
oil for deep-frying
1 tablespoon sesame oil
1 teaspoon red chilli flakes

1 tablespoon sugar
salt to taste
1 tablespoon sesame seeds, toasted

Method

1   Trim, wash, drain and pat spinach leaves dry. Cut into thin strips.

2   Heat oil in a wok; add spinach and deep-fry till crisp. Drain on absorbent paper.

3   Heat sesame oil in a separate wok; add red chilli flakes and immediately add fried spinach. Sprinkle salt to taste, sugar and toasted sesame seeds. Toss well to mix. Serve immediately.

CHEF'S TIP

As spinach has a high water content, first add a small quantity of spinach to stabilise the temperature of the oil before adding the rest.

KIMCHI

Ingredients

1 small cabbage, cut into 1-inch pieces

2 tablespoons sesame oil

4 teaspoons brown sugar

1 teaspoon light soy sauce

2 tablespoons white vinegar

3 teaspoons crushed dried red chillies

salt to taste

½ teaspoon sesame seeds, roasted

Method

1   Heat oil in a pan. Add brown sugar, soy sauce, vinegar, red chillies and salt to taste.

2   Add cabbage and turn off the heat. Toss well to mix. Sprinkle with roasted sesame seeds and serve immediately.

Note: This Korean dish is a very popular starter in Chinese restaurants.

SICHUAN CHILLI POTATOES

Ingredients

4-5 medium potatoes

3 tablespoons cornflour

2 tablespoons oil + for deep-frying

4-5 dried red chillies, broken into bits

8-10 Sichuan peppers (optional), crushed

1 medium onion, sliced

5-6 garlic cloves, finely chopped

1 teaspoon red chilli paste

1 teaspoon light soy sauce

½ teaspoon sugar

salt to taste

1 tablespoon brown vinegar

1 stalk spring onion greens, roughly chopped

Method

1   Peel and cut each potato into ten to twelve thick wedges. Soak wedges in cold water for half an hour. Heat water in a pan and parboil potatoes. Drain and cool.

2   Dust the parboiled potatoes with one-and-a-half tablespoons of cornflour.

3   Heat oil in a wok and deep-fry the potato wedges for two minutes, or until completely cooked, golden brown and crisp. Drain on absorbent paper. Mix the remaining cornflour and a quarter cup of water.

4   Heat two tablespoons of oil in a wok; add red chillies and stir-fry for half a minute. Add Sichuan peppers, onion and garlic and continue to stir-fry.

5   Stir in red chilli paste mixed with two tablespoons of water, soy sauce, sugar and salt to taste; stir-fry for half a minute.

6   Add fried potatoes and toss till heated through.

7   Stir in cornflour mixture, toss well to mix and add vinegar. Stir-fry for half a minute and serve immediately, garnished with spring onion greens.

PICKLED CUCUMBERS

Ingredients

4 small cucumbers

salt to taste

2 tablespoons white vinegar

2 teaspoons caster sugar

1 teaspoon sesame oil

1 fresh red chilli, halved

Method

1. Wash and halve unpeeled cucumbers. Remove seeds and cut into quarter-inch thick sticks.

2. Heat vinegar, caster sugar and sesame oil in a pan. When the mixture comes to a boil turn off the heat and add the cucumbers and salt and mix well.

3. Add the fresh red chilli and toss well to mix.

SESAME CORN TOAST

Ingredients

½ cup toasted sesame seeds
1 cup fresh corn kernels, finely minced
3 medium potatoes
1 medium green capsicum, finely chopped
1 medium onion, finely chopped
1 inch ginger, finely chopped
4-6 garlic cloves, finely chopped
2-3 green chillies, seeded and
    finely chopped
2 tablespoons fresh coriander leaves,
    finely chopped
½ tablespoon soy sauce
½ cup cornflour

½ teaspoon white pepper powder
¼ teaspoon MSG (optional)
salt to taste
8 bread slices
oil for deep-frying

Method

1   Boil potatoes; cool, peel and mash them in a deep bowl.

2   Add minced corn, green capsicum, onion, ginger, garlic, green chillies, coriander leaves, soy sauce, two tablespoons of cornflour, white pepper powder, MSG and salt; mix thoroughly.

3   Mix the remaining cornflour and half a cup of water. Cut bread slices with a round cutter into one-inch circles.

4   Brush each bread circle with the cornflour mixture; spread a thick layer of the corn mixture over it, smoothening the top with moistened fingers.

5   Sprinkle sesame seeds generously over the top and press lightly. Shake off excess seeds and refrigerate the corn and bread rounds for fifteen minutes.

6   Heat oil in a wok; deep-fry the rounds for two to three minutes, or until crisp and golden brown, turning occasionally.

7   Drain on absorbent paper. Serve hot with a sauce of your choice.

VEGETABLE SPRING ROLLS

Ingredients

Spring Roll Wrappers
¼ cup refined flour (*maida*)
1 cup + 1 tablespoon cornflour
salt to taste
oil

Filling
2 tablespoons oil + for deep-frying
1 medium onion, thinly sliced

2 medium carrots, grated
1 medium green capsicum, cut into thin strips
½ small cabbage, finely shredded
1 tablespoon light soy sauce
¼ teaspoon white pepper powder
salt to taste
¾ cup bean sprouts
2 spring onions, finely sliced

Method

1   To make the filling, heat two tablespoons of oil in a wok; add sliced onion and carrots and stir-fry for half a minute. Add green capsicum and cabbage and continue to stir-fry for one minute. Add soy sauce, white pepper powder and salt.

2   Add bean sprouts and sliced spring onions with the greens, and stir-fry for about half a minute. Remove from heat and cool the filling to room temperature.

3   To make spring roll wrappers, mix one cup of cornflour, the refined flour and salt to taste in a mixing bowl. Add two cups of water and whisk thoroughly. Strain the batter and set aside for fifteen minutes. Adjust the consistency of the batter by adding a little water if required.

4   Heat an eight-inch non-stick frying pan; brush with a little oil and pour a ladleful of batter into it. Swirl to coat the bottom of the pan and pour the excess batter back into the bowl. Cook over moderate heat till the edges start curling. Peel off or remove in one swift motion. Cool and sprinkle with a little cornflour. Repeat the process to make eight to ten wrappers.

5   Mix one tablespoon of cornflour and two tablespoons of water to make a paste.

6   Divide filling into eight to ten equal portions. Place a portion of filling at one end of each wrapper and roll tightly, folding the sides in while you roll. Seal the ends with the cornflour paste.

7   Heat oil in a wok; deep-fry two spring rolls at a time turning frequently, till crisp and golden brown. Drain on absorbent paper.

8   Cut each spring roll into four pieces and serve hot with Sichuan Sauce (*page 102*).

CANTONESE VEGETABLES

Ingredients

10-12 baby corn cobs, sliced diagonally

16-20 French beans, sliced diagonally

2 large carrots, sliced

2 small zucchini, sliced

2 large green capsicums
   cut into1-inch pieces

2 slices tinned bamboo shoots

8 tablespoons cornflour

4 tablespoons oil + for deep-frying

3 one-inch pieces ginger, thinly sliced

2 celery stalks, sliced

4 spring onions, sliced

1 tablespoon light soy sauce

¼ teaspoon MSG (optional)

¾ teaspoon white pepper powder

¾ teaspoon sugar

salt to taste

½ cup white wine (optional)

1½ cups Vegetable Stock (*page 104*)

Method

1   Toss the vegetables in six tablespoons of cornflour. Heat oil in a wok till it reaches smoking point. Add the vegetables to the hot oil and remove them almost immediately before they change colour. Drain on absorbent paper. Mix the remaining cornflour and two tablespoons of water.

2   Boil the bamboo shoot slices in one cup of hot water for ten minutes (*see Note on page 17*). Drain and slice thinly.

3   Heat four tablespoons of oil in a wok or pan; add ginger, celery and spring onions and stir-fry for a few seconds. Add bamboo shoots and continue to stir-fry for half a minute.

4   Add soy sauce, MSG, white pepper powder, sugar, salt to taste, white wine and the stock. Bring to a boil, lower heat and simmer for three to four minutes. Add cornflour mixture and cook till the sauce thickens a little.

5   Add the fried vegetables and continue to simmer for one minute, stirring very gently. Serve hot.

TOFU IN HOT GARLIC SAUCE

Ingredients

400 grams bean curd (tofu) cut into
   1-inch cubes

3 tablespoons oil + for deep-frying

1 medium onion

2 tablespoons cornflour

2-3 dried red chillies, broken in half

20 garlic cloves, chopped

4 tablespoons tomato sauce

1 tablespoon white vinegar

2 tablespoons red chilli paste

1 tablespoon hot black bean paste

1 teaspoon sugar

salt to taste

1 cup Vegetable Stock (*page 104*)

½ medium green capsicum, cut into
   ½-inch diamonds

½ medium red or yellow capsicum,
   cut into ½-inch diamonds

1 spring onion, finely sliced

1 tablespoon sesame oil

1 tablespoon red chilli flakes

Method

1   Heat oil in a wok and deep-fry tofu for three to four minutes. Drain on absorbent paper.

2   Cut onion into quarters and separate each layer. Mix cornflour and one cup of water.

3   Heat three tablespoons of oil in a wok; add red chillies and garlic and stir-fry for half a minute.

4   Add tomato sauce, vinegar, red chilli paste, black bean paste, sugar and salt. Stir in vegetable stock and continue to cook on high heat for one minute.

5   Add green and red capsicums, onion and spring onion and cook for a couple of minutes more. Stir in cornflour mixture and cook till the sauce starts to thicken.

6   Add deep-fried tofu and toss well to coat with the sauce.

7   Drizzle with sesame oil, sprinkle red chilli flakes and serve hot.

EIGHT - JEWEL VEGETABLES

Ingredients

¼ small head broccoli, separated
 into florets

1 small carrot, cut into ½-inch cubes

1 small red capsicum, cut into
 ½-inch pieces

1 small yellow capsicum, cut into
 ½-inch pieces

1 small green capsicum, cut into
 ½-inch pieces

1 small zucchini, cut into ½-inch pieces

5-6 fresh button mushrooms, halved

3 tablespoons oil

10-12 cashew nuts

salt to taste

3 spring onions, sliced

3-4 garlic cloves, chopped

1 inch ginger, chopped

2 fresh red chillies, sliced

1 tablespoon black bean sauce

2 teaspoons rice wine (optional)

1 tablespoon dark soy sauce

1 teaspoon brown sugar

¼ teaspoon MSG (optional)

2 teaspoons cornflour

1 teaspoon sesame oil

Method

1 Blanch broccoli and carrot separately in boiling water for a few minutes. Drain, refresh in cold water and set aside.

2 Heat one tablespoon of oil in a pan and fry cashew nuts till light golden. Drain on absorbent paper.

3 Heat two tablespoons of oil in a wok until almost smoking. Add spring onions, garlic and ginger and sauté on medium heat for half a minute.

4 Add sliced red chillies, red, yellow and green capsicums, zucchini and mushrooms and stir-fry for two minutes.

5 Add broccoli, carrot, black bean sauce, rice wine, soy sauce, brown sugar and MSG together with two tablespoons of water; continue to stir-fry for another two minutes. Stir in the cornflour mixed with four teaspoons of water.

6 Add the fried cashew nuts and sesame oil; adjust seasoning and toss to mix well. Serve hot.

SICHUAN VEGETABLES

Ingredients

½ medium head broccoli, separated
   into small florets

8-10 snow peas, halved

4-6 fresh button mushrooms, sliced

1 medium red capsicum, cut into
   1-inch pieces

1 medium yellow capsicum, cut into
   1-inch pieces

1 medium green capsicum, cut into
   1-inch pieces

3 tablespoons oil

4-5 garlic cloves, crushed

2 spring onions, chopped

1 celery stalk, finely chopped

1½ tablespoons red chilli paste

8-10 Sichuan peppers (optional)

1 teaspoon sugar

salt to taste

¼ teaspoon MSG (optional)

2 cups Vegetable Stock (*page 104*)

3 tablespoons cornflour

1 tablespoon white vinegar

Method

1 Heat oil in a wok or pan; add garlic, spring onions and celery and stir-fry for one minute. Add red chilli paste, Sichuan peppers, sugar, salt and MSG. Add half a cup of vegetable stock and cook for one minute.

2 Add broccoli florets, snow peas, mushrooms, red, yellow and green capsicums and stir-fry for two minutes. Stir in remaining vegetable stock and cook on high heat for a couple of minutes.

3 Mix cornflour and one cup of water and stir into the pan. Cook on medium heat for one minute until the sauce starts to thicken, stirring occasionally.

4 Stir in vinegar and mix well. Serve hot.

SIZZLING TOFU WITH ASSORTED VEGETABLES

Ingredients

200 grams bean curd (tofu)

6 French beans, cut into 1-inch pieces

1 medium carrot, cut into 1-inch cubes

½ medium cabbage, cut into 1-inch pieces

1 medium green capsicum, cut
   into 1-inch pieces

salt to taste

a pinch of five-spice powder

2 tablespoons sugar

2 teaspoons garlic paste

1 teaspoon ginger paste

2 tablespoons oil + for shallow-frying

2 medium onions, sliced

2 tablespoons red chilli sauce

¼ teaspoon white pepper powder

a pinch of MSG (optional)

1 tablespoon cornflour

1 tablespoon white vinegar

Method

1. Cut tofu into thick triangles, each side measuring one-and-a-half inches.

2. Mix together salt, five-spice powder, sugar, garlic paste and ginger paste and two tablespoons of water in a shallow plate. Roll the tofu triangles in the spice mixture to coat thoroughly, and marinate for one hour, preferably in a refrigerator.

3. Preheat the sizzler plate. Heat oil in a pan and shallow-fry the marinated tofu for two to three minutes until golden brown. Drain on absorbent paper.

4. Heat two tablespoons of oil in a wok. Add onions, French beans and carrot and stir-fry. Add cabbage, green capsicum, salt and red chilli sauce and mix well. Add white pepper powder and MSG.

5. Mix cornflour and a quarter cup of water and add to the stir-fried vegetables. Cook for one minute.

6. Place the hot sizzler plate on its wooden base. Arrange the fried tofu on the hot plate, top with the vegetables, sprinkle some vinegar and serve immediately.

CHEF'S TIP

If you do not have a sizzler plate, serve the tofu in a bowl topped with the hot stir-fried vegetables.

MIXED VEGETABLE MANCHURIAN

Ingredients

1 medium cabbage, grated
1 medium carrot, grated
8-10 French beans, finely chopped
salt to taste
3 medium spring onions, finely chopped
1 medium green capsicum, finely chopped
¼ cup refined flour (*maida*)
¼ cup cornflour
oil for deep-frying

Sauce

2 tablespoons oil
1 inch ginger, finely chopped

4-6 garlic cloves, finely chopped
2-inch celery stalk, finely chopped
3 green chillies, finely chopped
2 tablespoons light soy sauce
1 teaspoon sugar
¼ teaspoon MSG (optional)
salt to taste
2½ cups Vegetable Stock (*page 104*)
3 tablespoons cornflour
1 tablespoon white vinegar

Method

1 Mix chopped cabbage, carrot and French beans in a bowl and thoroughly rub in one teaspoon of salt. Add spring onions, reserving some for garnishing, green capsicum, refined flour and one-fourth cup of cornflour. Mix thoroughly and shape into lemon-sized balls.

2 Heat oil in a wok; deep-fry vegetable balls in small batches for three to four minutes on medium heat until golden brown. Drain on absorbent paper.

3 Heat two tablespoons of oil in a wok or a pan; stir-fry the ginger and garlic for one minute. Add celery and green chillies and stir-fry for one minute more. Add soy sauce, sugar, MSG and salt; stir in vegetable stock and bring to a boil.

4 Mix three tablespoons of cornflour and one cup of water and stir into the hot stock. Cook, stirring continuously, for a couple of minutes or until the sauce starts to thicken.

5 Add the fried vegetable balls and vinegar and stir gently to mix. Serve hot, garnished with chopped spring onions.

CHEF'S TIP

To serve the dish without the sauce, reduce the stock to one cup and the cornflour in the sauce to one-and-a-half tablespoons.

MIXED VEGETABLES
IN BLACK PEPPER

Ingredients

½ small head broccoli, separated
   into florets

1 medium carrot, sliced

1 medium red capsicum,cut into
   thick strips

1 medium green capsicum,
   cut into thick strips

10-12 snow peas, halved

6 fresh button mushrooms, quartered

2 tablespoons oil

2-3 garlic cloves, crushed

8-10 black peppercorns, crushed

2 teaspoons light soy sauce

salt to taste

¼ teaspoon MSG (optional)

½ teaspoon sugar

2 tablespoons cornflour

Method

1   Blanch broccoli and carrots in boiling salted water for one minute. Drain, refresh in cold water, drain again and set aside.

2   Heat oil in a wok; add garlic and stir-fry for one minute.

3   Add broccoli and carrot and stir-fry for two minutes. Add red and green capsicums, snow peas and mushrooms and continue to stir-fry for another two minutes.

4   Add crushed pepper, soy sauce, salt, MSG and sugar and cook on high heat for two minutes, stirring and tossing continuously.

5   Mix cornflour with one-and-a-half cups of water and add to the wok. Cook, stirring continuously, for one minute or till the sauce thickens.

6   Serve hot.

SWEET AND SOUR VEGETABLES

Ingredients

8-10 French beans, cut into 1-inch pieces
½ medium head broccoli, separated
    into florets
1 medium carrot, sliced diagonally
6-8 baby corn cobs, cut diagonally
    into ½-inch slices
2 medium onions
1 medium green capsicum, cut
    into 1-inch squares
6 fresh button mushrooms, quartered
2 slices tinned pineapple, cut into
    ½-inch pieces

3 tablespoons tomato ketchup
2 tablespoons sugar
¼ teaspoon MSG (optional)
½ teaspoon white pepper powder
salt to taste
1½ cups Vegetable Stock (*page 104*)
3 tablespoons cornflour
2 tablespoons oil
½ inch ginger, chopped
2-3 garlic cloves, chopped
3 tablespoons white vinegar

Method

1   Blanch French beans, broccoli, carrot and baby corn separately in boiling water for two minutes. Drain and refresh in cold water. Cut onions into quarters and separate the layers.

2   Blend tomato sauce, sugar, MSG, white pepper powder and salt in one cup of vegetable stock. Mix cornflour in one cup of water and set aside.

3   Heat two tablespoons of oil in a wok; add ginger and garlic and stir-fry for one minute. Add onion and continue to stir-fry for one minute. Add green capsicum and mushrooms and stir-fry for two minutes. Add blanched French beans, broccoli, carrot and baby corn and continue to stir-fry for another minute.

4   Stir in the sauce and spice mix, remaining vegetable stock and cornflour mixture and cook on low heat for two to three minutes, or until the sauce starts to thicken, stirring continuously.

5   Add pineapple pieces and cook for one minute more. Stir in the vinegar and serve hot.

CRISP NOODLES WITH STIR-FRIED VEGETABLES

Ingredients

200 grams eggless noodles

2 medium carrots, cut into ½-inch diamonds

2 medium green capsicums,
   cut into ½-inch diamonds

½ small head broccoli, separated
   into small florets

6 baby corn cobs, sliced diagonally

salt to taste

3 tablespoons oil + for deep-frying

2-3 garlic cloves, finely chopped

1 inch ginger, finely chopped

1 medium onion, sliced

1 celery stalk, finely chopped

1 fresh red chilli, sliced diagonally

1 tablespoon dark soy sauce

½ teaspoon white pepper powder

½ teaspoon MSG (optional)

2¼ cups Vegetable Stock (*page 104*)

2 tablespoons cornflour

¼ cup bean sprouts

Method

1   Boil noodles in six to eight cups of salted water to which one tablespoon of oil has been added; cook till almost done. Drain, refresh in cold water, drain again and spread on a large plate to cool.

2   Heat oil in a wok and deep-fry noodles till crisp and golden brown. Drain on absorbent paper.

3   Heat two tablespoons of oil in a wok; add garlic and ginger and sauté on moderate heat for half a minute. Add onion, celery and red chilli and continue to sauté for another minute.

4   Add carrots, green capsicums, broccoli and baby corn; sauté on high heat for two to three minutes, stirring and tossing continuously.

5   Add soy sauce, white pepper powder, MSG and salt to taste and sauté for one minute. Stir in the vegetable stock and bring to a boil.

6   Mix cornflour and three tablespoons of water and stir into the vegetables. Simmer for two to three minutes, stirring continuously till sauce is thick and clear. Add bean sprouts and toss to mix.

7   Arrange the fried noodles in a serving plate or a large bowl, spoon the vegetables on top and serve immediately.

PAN-FRIED NOODLES

Ingredients

200 grams eggless noodles
salt to taste
4 tablespoons oil + for deep-frying
1 inch ginger, sliced
6-8 garlic cloves, chopped
2 spring onion bulbs, sliced
4-6 fresh button mushrooms, sliced
½ medium bunch (100 grams) spinach,
    shredded
1 medium green capsicum, cut into
    ½-inch pieces
½ medium red capsicum, cut into
    ½-inch pieces

¼ small cabbage, finely shredded
½ teaspoon white pepper powder
¼ teaspoon MSG (optional)
1 tablespoon light soy sauce
4-5 black peppercorns, crushed
1½ cups Vegetable Stock (*page 104*)
2 tablespoons cornflour
2 cups bean sprouts
1 teaspoon white vinegar

Method

1   Boil noodles in six to eight cups of salted water to which one tablespoon of oil has been added; cook till almost done. Drain and refresh in cold water. Drain again and spread on a large plate to cool.

2   Heat oil in a frying pan and gently arrange the noodles in it. Press noodles using a spatula or the back of a large spoon. Cook on medium heat till noodles are crisp on the underside and take the shape of the pan. Remove and drain on absorbent paper. Keep warm.

3   Heat three tablespoons of oil in a wok; add ginger and sauté till brown. Add garlic and sauté for one minute.

4   Add spring onions, mushrooms and spinach and sauté for two minutes. Add green capsicum, red capsicum and cabbage and stir well. Add salt, white pepper powder, MSG, soy sauce, crushed peppercorns and vegetable stock.

5   Stir in cornflour mixed with two tablespoons of water. Cook for another two minutes till the sauce is thick and bubbling. Add bean sprouts and vinegar and mix well; adjust seasoning.

6   Place the noodle cake on a plate; pour the steaming hot vegetables over the noodles and serve immediately.

PINEAPPLE FRIED RICE

Ingredients

3-4 slices tinned pineapple, finely chopped

1½ cups rice, soaked

salt to taste

2 tablespoons oil

4 spring onions, finely chopped

2 green chillies, seeded and chopped

1 small carrot, grated

6-8 French beans, sliced

1 teaspoon light soy sauce

¼ teaspoon MSG (optional)

1 fresh red chilli, seeded and sliced into thin strips

Method

1   Cook rice in four cups of boiling salted water till almost done. Drain, refresh in cold water and drain again. Spread on a large plate to cool.

2   Heat oil in a wok; add spring onions and green chillies and stir-fry for one minute.

3   Add carrot and French beans and continue to stir-fry for another two minutes.

4   Add rice, soy sauce, MSG and salt to taste and sauté for two minutes, stirring and tossing continuously. Add pineapple and continue to sauté for one minute.

5   Garnish with the fresh red chilli and serve hot, preferably in a freshly scooped out pineapple shell.

QUICK STIR-FRIED NOODLES

Ingredients

200 grams eggless noodles

salt to taste

3 tablespoons oil

1 medium onion, sliced

1 medium carrot, cut into thin strips

¼ medium cabbage, shredded

1 medium green capsicum, cut into thin strips

2 stalks spring onion greens, sliced diagonally

1½ tablespoons light soy sauce

1 cup bean sprouts

1 teaspoon sesame oil

Method

1   Boil noodles in six to eight cups of salted water to which one tablespoon of oil has been added; cook till almost done. Drain, refresh in cold water and drain again. Spread on a large plate to cool.

2   Heat two tablespoons of oil in a wok to smoking point. Add onion and stir-fry for one minute. Add carrot, cabbage and green capsicum and stir-fry for two to three minutes.

3   Add noodles and salt; stir and toss for one more minute.

4   Add spring onion greens and soy sauce and toss again. Add bean sprouts and toss well.

5   Transfer the noodles to a serving bowl, sprinkle sesame oil over and serve immediately.

TRIPLE SICHUAN RICE

Ingredients

100 grams eggless noodles

salt to taste

2½ tablespoons oil + for deep-frying

1½ cups Singapore noodles (*page 80*)

2 medium onions, finely chopped

4 tablespoons Sichuan sauce (*page 102*)

1½ cups Vegetable Fried Rice (*page 82*)

3 tablespoons Hot Garlic Sauce (*page 98*)

2 teaspoons cornflour

½ cup Vegetable Stock (*page 104*)

2 stalks spring onion greens, finely shredded

Method

1 Boil noodles in six cups of salted water to which half a tablespoon of oil has been added and cook till almost done. Drain, refresh in cold water, drain again and spread on a large plate to cool.

2 Heat oil in a wok and deep-fry noodles till crisp and golden brown. Drain on absorbent paper.

3   Heat one tablespoon of oil in a wok; add half the onions and stir-fry for a few seconds. Add Singapore Noodles and one tablespoon of Sichuan Sauce and cook on high heat for two minutes, stirring and tossing continuously until noodles are heated through. Transfer to a bowl and keep warm.

4   Heat one tablespoon of oil in the same wok; add the remaining onions and stir-fry for a few seconds. Add Vegetable Fried Rice and one tablespoon of Sichuan Sauce and cook on high heat for two minutes, stirring and tossing continuously. Transfer to another bowl and keep warm.

5   Heat three tablespoons of Hot Garlic Sauce in a pan. Mix two teaspoons of cornflour and half a cup of vegetable stock and add it to the pan. Cook till the mixture thickens, stirring continuously.

6   Arrange Singapore noodles at the bottom of a large serving bowl, top with the vegetable fried rice and finally with the crisp fried noodles. Pour the thick hot garlic sauce over the fried noodles, garnish with spring onion greens and serve hot.

BROCCOLI AND ZUCCHINI CHOWMEIN

Ingredients

½ small head broccoli, separated into florets

1 medium zucchini, cut into thin strips

200 grams eggless noodles

salt to taste

3 tablespoons oil

6-8 baby corn cobs, halved

2-3 garlic cloves, sliced

1 inch ginger, finely chopped

1 medium onion, sliced

6 fresh medium button mushrooms, halved

1 medium red capsicum, cut into thin strips

2 teaspoons light soy sauce

¼ teaspoon MSG (optional)

2 teaspoons cornflour

1 teaspoon sesame oil

1 tablespoon toasted sesame seeds

Method

1   Boil noodles in six to eight cups of salted water to which one tablespoon of oil has been added, and cook till almost done. Drain, refresh in cold water, drain again and spread on a large plate to cool.

2   Blanch broccoli and baby corn separately in boiling water for two minutes. Drain, refresh in cold water and set aside.

3   Heat two tablespoons of oil in a wok; add garlic, ginger and onion and stir-fry for two minutes.

4   Add blanched broccoli and baby corn, mushrooms, red capsicum and zucchini and stir-fry for another two minutes.

5   Stir in the soy sauce, MSG and salt. Mix cornflour and two tablespoons of water and add to the vegetables, stirring until the sauce thickens.

6   Add noodles and sesame oil; toss to mix well and cook on low heat for two to three minutes until noodles are warmed through.

7   Serve hot, garnished with toasted sesame seeds.

SOFT NOODLES

Ingredients

200 grams eggless noodles
salt to taste
3 tablespoons oil
3 spring onions, sliced

2 one-inch pieces ginger, cut into fine strips
1 teaspoon light soy sauce
7-8 black peppercorns, freshly ground
2 stalks spring onion greens, sliced

Method

1   Boil noodles in plenty of salted water to which one tablespoon of oil has been
    added, and cook till soft. Drain, refresh in cold water, drain again and spread on a
    large plate to cool.

2   Heat the remaining oil in a wok. Add spring onions and stir-fry for half a minute.
    Add ginger strips and stir-fry for half a minute more. Add the boiled noodles and soy
    sauce and stir gently to separate each noodle.

3   Add salt and crushed peppercorns and mix gently.Garnish with spring onion greens
    and serve hot.

SINGAPORE NOODLES

Ingredients

200 grams rice noodles

salt to taste

1 tablespoon oil

4 tablespoons Chilli Oil (*page 100*)

1 inch ginger, chopped

3-4 garlic cloves, chopped

¼ small cabbage, finely shredded

1 small carrot, grated

1 medium green capsicum,
   cut into thin strips

2 spring onions, sliced

½ tablespoon light soy sauce

3 tablespoons tomato sauce

¼ teaspoon MSG (optional)

½ teaspoon white pepper powder

½ cup bean sprouts

1 tablespoon white vinegar

Method

1   Boil six cups of water in a deep pan. Add salt and one tablespoon of oil. Add the noodles; take the pan off the heat, cover and leave to stand for three minutes. Drain noodles, refresh in cold water and drain again. Spread on a large plate to cool.

2   Heat chilli oil in a wok; add ginger and garlic and stir-fry for one minute. Add cabbage, carrot and capsicum and continue to stir-fry for one minute. Add spring onions, reserving some greens for garnishing, and cook on high heat for one minute more.

3   Add noodles, soy sauce, tomato sauce, MSG, white pepper powder and salt to taste. Mix well and cook for a couple of minutes, tossing and stirring continuously.

4   Add the bean sprouts and vinegar and toss well. Serve hot, garnished with reserved spring onion greens.

VEGETABLE FRIED RICE

Ingredients

1½ cups rice

12-15 French beans, sliced

1 medium carrot, finely chopped

1 medium green capsicum, finely chopped

¼ medium cabbage, chopped

4 tablespoons oil

3-4 garlic cloves, finely chopped

salt to taste

1 teaspoon light soy sauce

¼ teaspoon MSG (optional)

½ teaspoon white pepper powder

½ tablespoon white vinegar

2 spring onion greens, sliced

Method

1   Soak rice in four to five cups of water for one hour. Cook in five cups of water until just cooked. Drain and spread on a plate to cool.

2   Heat oil in a wok; add garlic and stir-fry for one minute. Add French beans, carrot, green capsicum and cabbage and stir-fry for two minutes.

3   Add cooked rice and salt and cook for one minute, stirring continuously. Add soy sauce, MSG and white pepper powder and mix thoroughly.

4   Stir in the vinegar. Garnish with spring onion greens and serve hot.

CHILLI GARLIC NOODLES

Ingredients

200 grams eggless noodles

salt to taste

1 tablespoon oil

3 tablespoons Chilli Oil (*page 100*)

1 medium onion, sliced

12-15 garlic cloves, sliced

3 fresh red chillies, thinly sliced

3 stalks spring onion greens, finely chopped

1 teaspoon red chilli sauce

¼ teaspoon MSG (optional)

1 teaspoon white vinegar

1 cup bean sprouts

Method

1   Boil noodles in six to eight cups of salted water to which one tablespoon of oil has been added; cook till almost done. Drain, refresh in cold water. Drain again and spread on a large plate to cool.

2   Heat two tablespoons of chilli oil in a wok; add onion, garlic and red chillies reserving a few slices for garnishing, and stir-fry for two minutes.

3   Add noodles, spring onion greens, red chilli sauce, MSG, vinegar and salt and cook for two minutes, stirring and tossing continuously, until noodles are heated through.

4   Add bean sprouts and the remaining chilli oil and toss to mix.

5   Serve, garnished with the reserved red chillies.

HAKKA-STYLE RICE NOODLES

Ingredients

150 grams rice noodles

salt to taste

4 tablespoons oil

1 medium onion, sliced

1 small carrot, cut into thin strips

1 medium green capsicum, cut into thin strips

6-8 French beans, cut into thin strips

¼ small cabbage, finely shredded

1 tablespoon light soy sauce

¼ teaspoon MSG (optional)

¼ teaspoon white pepper powder

½ cup bean sprouts

1 stalk spring onion greens, cut into fine long strips

Method

1   Boil six cups of water in a deep pan. Add salt and one tablespoon of oil. Add the noodles, take the pan off the heat, cover and leave to stand for three minutes. Drain noodles, refresh in cold water and drain again. Spread on a large plate to cool.

2   Heat remaining oil in a wok; add onion and stir-fry for two minutes.

3   Add carrot, green capsicum, French beans and cabbage and stir-fry for two minutes, stirring and tossing continuously.

4   Add noodles, soy sauce, MSG, salt to taste and white pepper powder; cook on high heat for a couple of minutes, tossing continuously, until noodles are heated through.

5   Add bean sprouts, mix well and serve hot, garnished with spring onion greens.

ALMOND PUDDING

Ingredients

15 grams agar-agar (China grass)

1¾ cups milk

1¼ cups sugar

1½ teaspoons almond essence

Method

1 Cut agar-agar strands into one-inch pieces. Soak in two-and-a-half cups of cold water for eight hours. Do not stir.

2 Transfer the agar-agar, together with the water, to a saucepan and bring to a boil. Lower heat and simmer until the agar-agar has dissolved completely.

3 Heat milk in a seprate pan; when it comes to a boil, add it to the agar-agar mixture. Add sugar and stir. Cook gently for ten minutes more.

4 Stir in the almond essence. Take the pan off the heat, and pour the contents into an eight-and-a-half inch by six-and-a-half inch shallow (one-inch deep) tray, and fill to the rim.

5 The agar-agar will set at room temperature. When firm, cut into cubes and serve.

BAKED COCONUT RICE PUDDING

Ingredients

1/3 cup short or round grain rice

2½ cups coconut milk

1¼ cups milk

1 large strip lemon rind

½ cup caster sugar

1½ tablespoons butter

a pinch of ground star anise (*chakri phool/badiyan*)

Method

1   Lightly grease a shallow ovenproof dish. Preheat the oven to 180°C.

2   Mix rice with coconut milk, milk, lemon rind and caster sugar. Transfer the mixture to the greased dish. Dot the surface with butter and bake for about half an hour.

3   Take the dish out of the oven. Remove the lemon rind, add a pinch of ground star anise and mix gently.

4   Return the dish to the oven and bake for sixty to ninety minutes, or until almost all the milk has been absorbed and the top turns a golden brown.

5   Serve the pudding warm or chilled with a choice of seasonal fresh or stewed fruit.

CHEF'S TIP

If the top turns golden before the end of the cooking time, cover the dish with aluminium foil to avoid excessive browning.

DAARSAAN

Ingredients

16-20 Wonton Wrappers *(page 26)*
oil for deep-frying
1 tablespoon butter
¼ cup sugar

¼ cup honey
2 tablespoons sesame seeds, toasted
2 tablespoons icing sugar

Method

1   Make eight to ten long slits in the wonton wrappers leaving the edges intact. Moisten top and bottom edges, roll loosely as you would a toffee wrapper. Pinch the ends to secure.

2   Heat oil in a wok; deep-fry the wonton wrappers for one minute, or until crisp and golden brown. Drain on absorbent paper and transfer to a shallow serving dish. Keep warm.

3   Heat butter in a pan with one tablespoon of water and sugar. Cook until sugar melts and turns a light golden brown. Lower heat and stir in the honey. Pour the hot sauce over the fried wontons. Sprinkle with toasted sesame seeds and icing sugar and serve warm.

TOFFEE LYCHEES

Ingredients

16 large tinned lychees

½ cup refined flour (*maida*)

2 tablespoons cornflour

¼ teaspoon baking powder

oil for deep-frying

1 tablespoon butter

½ cup sugar

1 teaspoon sesame seeds, toasted

Method

1   Sift refined flour, cornflour and baking powder together. Gradually stir in one-third cup of water and whisk to make a smooth batter.

2   Heat oil in a wok; dip lychees in the batter and deep-fry for about one minute, or until light golden brown, turning over a few times. Drain on absorbent paper and keep warm.

3   Heat butter in a pan; add two tablespoons of water and sugar. Cook until sugar melts and turns light golden brown.

4   Take the pan off the heat and dip fried lychees in the hot caramel. Sprinkle with toasted sesame seeds and dip quickly in iced water to harden the caramel. Serve immediately.

DATE AND WALNUT WONTONS

Ingredients

100 grams seedless dates, finely chopped
½ cup walnuts kernels
16 Wonton Wrappers (*page26*)

2 tablespoons brown sugar
¼ teaspoon cinnamon powder
oil for deep-frying

Method

1   Boil walnut kernels in two cups of water for one minute. Drain, pat dry and chop coarsely.

2   Mix dates, walnuts, brown sugar and cinnamon powder. Divide the mixture into sixteen equal portions.

3   Place a portion of date and walnut mixture in the centre of each wonton wrapper and moisten the edges with a little water. Fold the wrapper in half, twist the edges and press down to stick.

4   Heat oil in a wok; deep-fry wontons for a couple of minutes or until golden brown and crisp. Drain on absorbent paper. Serve hot with ice cream.

HOT GARLIC SAUCE

Ingredients

2 tablespoons oil

2-3 dried red chillies

1 spring onion, finely chopped

10-12 garlic cloves, finely chopped

4 tablespoons tomato sauce

1 tablespoon white vinegar

2 tablespoons red chilli paste

1 tablespoon hot black bean paste

1 teaspoon sugar

salt to taste

1 cup Vegetable Stock (*page 104*)

2 tablespoons cornflour

Method

1 Heat oil in a wok or pan; add red chillies, spring onions and garlic and stir-fry for one minute.

2 Add tomato sauce, vinegar, chilli paste, black bean paste, sugar and salt to taste.

3 Stir in vegetable stock and continue to cook on high heat for one minute.

4 Mix the cornflour and one cup of water and stir into the sauce.

5 Cook till the sauce starts to thicken, stirring continuously.

CHEF'S TIP

This wonderfully tasty sauce has a short shelf life, so use immediately.

CHILLI OIL

Ingredients
1¼ cups groundnut oil
6 tablespoons chopped dried red chillies
2-3 teaspoons red chilli powder
1-2 tablespoons sesame oil

Method

1. Heat oil in a wok. Add red chillies and cook on low heat for at least ten minutes. Set aside to cool.

2. When completely cold, stir in the red chilli powder and sesame oil. Cover and leave to stand for at least twelve hours.

3. Strain into a sterilised bottle and store in a cool, dark place.

Chilli Oil - Flavoured Hot And Sour Vegetable Sc

SICHUAN SAUCE

Ingredients

10-12 dried red chillies

½ cup oil

10 garlic cloves, finely chopped

2 green chillies, finely chopped

2 spring onions, finely chopped

1 inch ginger, grated

2-3 inch celery stalk, finely chopped

3 tablespoons tomato ketchup

salt to taste

2 teaspoons white vinegar

Method

1   Remove stems and boil red chillies in one cup of water for five to seven minutes. Drain chillies, cool and grind to a fine paste.

2   Heat oil in a pan; add garlic, green chillies, spring onions and ginger and sauté for one minute. Add red chilli paste and continue to sauté for a few more seconds. Add celery, tomato ketchup and salt and stir well to mix.

3   Stir in the vinegar and simmer for one minute. When the oil rises to the surface, take the pan off the heat.

4   Cool, bottle and store.

5   Sichuan sauce will keep for a month if there is oil covering the surface.

VEGETABLE STOCK

Ingredients

1 medium onion, sliced

½ medium carrot, sliced

2-3 inch celery stalk, chopped

2 garlic cloves, crushed

1 bay leaf

5-6 black peppercorns

2-3 cloves

Method

1   Put all the ingredients into a pan with five cups of water and bring to a boil. Simmer for fifteen minutes and strain Cool and store in a refrigerator.

2   Vegetable stock will keep for two to three days in a refrigerator.